THE GODDESS WHO CHOSE ME

HOW I FOUND HEAVEN IN HER EYES

HARSHA & SAMEER NAGI

Made with ♥ on the Notion Press Platform
www.notionpress.com

The time we got, seems short !

But the time we spent, feels long..

Long like ages,

Like we knew each other forever!

The journey we shared had all the flavours,

And what we truly found, is 'love', that is eternal!

With the blessings of our guiding angel Nanaji Shri Dada Sabhani ji, whose light has shone upon us.

The light that has got these words pour out into these stories of pure love & companionship.

Contents

Contents

Foreword

Some love stories are written in ink.

Ours was written in soul.

This book is not just a recollection of memories—it's a tribute to a love that found me, changed me, and still echoes through every heartbeat. It is the story of how two souls met in the ordinary world of lectures and libraries, but created something extraordinary—a connection that felt timeless, destined, and sacred.

She was more than my beloved. She was my teacher, my muse, my mirror—my goddess. And somehow, in a world full of uncertainties, she chose me.

As you turn these pages, you're not just reading a story. You're entering a journey—of friendship becoming devotion, of laughter laced with longing, and of love that whispered, "We've met before."

This is the beginning. Part one of a love that even time cannot contain.

-Sameer Nagi

Preface

Some stories begin with a moment.

Ours began with a feeling—one that neither of us could explain, yet both of us quietly recognized.

This book is the first chapter of a love story that continues to live within me. It traces the delicate beginning—when two young souls, unaware of what lay ahead, found each other during the vibrant, chaotic, and unforgettable days of post-graduation.

It was a time of discovery, ambition, and transformation—but above all, it was the time when I met her.

She wasn't just another person in a classroom. She was light in human form. She carried both depth and grace, mischief and wisdom, softness and strength. From the very beginning, she felt like home.

In these pages, I have tried not just to recall what happened, but to capture how it felt—to fall in love with her laughter, to hold sacred even the smallest moments, to realize that something eternal had quietly taken root between us.

This story is for anyone who has ever felt love touch them in a way that defied reason. For anyone who has looked into someone's eyes and thought, "There you are. I've been waiting."

The Goddess Who Chose Me is not a grand tale filled with drama and spectacle. It is something more intimate—a quiet unfolding of a deep, soulful connection between two people who didn't know where they were going, but knew they were meant to walk together.

This is just the beginning.

And yet, even the beginning felt like forever.
Dear Harsha,
Forever Yours, Sameer!

Acknowledgements

First and always, to her—

The soul who walked into my life and changed its rhythm forever.

This book exists because you existed in my life—with your laughter, your wisdom, your gentleness, and your fierce, unwavering love.

You are not just the reason this story was written—you are the story.

To the quiet moments we shared, the glances we exchanged, and the silences that said everything—thank you. Every word in these pages breathes because of those memories.

You gave me a love that words can only hope to capture.

To our families (Isranis, Nagis and Ramtanis), who are the bedrock of our life. Our journey challenged you too in ways beyond one could have imagined. You allowed it to be deep and meaningful. Our children Aleesha and Gauri - We love you!

To the readers who pick up this book with open hearts—thank you. If our story touches you in even the smallest way, then I've done justice to the love that inspired it.

And finally, to the divine, mysterious force that brought two souls together in a crowded world—I am endlessly grateful.

Some people wait lifetimes for a love like this. I was blessed to live it.

With love and reverence,
Sameer & his Goddess!

Prologue

We don't always recognize the most important moments of our lives while we're living them.

Sometimes, they begin quietly—with a smile across a classroom, a question asked in passing, or the way someone's presence feels strangely familiar, as if your soul has met theirs long before your body ever did.

That's how she entered my life.

Not with thunder, not with fanfare—just with a softness that settled deep into my being.

She was not just beautiful. She was divine in a way that couldn't be defined. A presence that made me pause, listen, and feel... truly feel.

In a world full of distractions, she became my stillness. In the noise of ambition and expectation, she became my clarity.

And though I didn't know it then, that was the moment my life quietly shifted into a before and after.

This book begins where we began—during our post-graduation days, when we were simply students sharing dreams and notes, unaware that we were also sharing something far more eternal.

What started as friendship became a connection deeper than logic could explain. It wasn't just love. It was recognition. As though two stars, long separated by lifetimes, had finally found their orbit again.

This is the story of that beginning.

Of when I met the goddess who chose me.

And of how, from that moment on, I was never truly the same.

1

Two Lonely Souls in a Café

During an early monsoon shower, two students, new to their post-graduate college, wandered through a large crowd on a big campus, heading to the café. Two lonely souls in a campus full of lively strangers began walking together.

A gentle nudge from fate brought them side by side.

They uttered shy 'hellos' to one another, exchanged smiles, and asked, "Where are you upto?"

Their destination was the same, and their desires aligned. Nescafé was peaceful, quiet, and tucked away in a lovely little space surrounded by huge, beautiful, and calming trees. The two souls opened up and realized the depth of their shared feelings of loneliness and struggle over the past three to four years. Both had learned to live alone among the people around them.

The desire for companionship, the wish for someone who understands, was mutual. They provided each other with something they had long yearned for: listening and understanding.

Both had left their families to join graduate college and found themselves living alone during those years. Their experiences were similar; their ways of processing reality mirrored one another. They both relished the Maggi at the café.

"When is your birthday?" asked the boy. The girl responded, "16th Dec."

"There you go, our birth dates are also close. Mine is on 15th December." It was an instant connection, as if Cupid had validated that "she is the one" by sending a hint with this last coincidence.

"I have felt this connection after years, probably for the first time," the boy thought.

As both happier souls walked back to their respective hostels, they saved each other's numbers, knowing they would want to meet again.

"Bye, Harsha. Bye, Sameer..." They exchanged friendly smiles as they parted ways, a joyful feeling in their hearts.

2

The Longing for Long Walks

"Hi, I am going for a walk. Want to come?" texted the boy.

The girl responded, "Yes, sure," smiling behind the screen.

Their hearts longed for the companionship offered through the exchanges of such messages. The monsoon showers had swept the streets clean, and the lush trees bowed down, making the evening strolls beautiful.

New campus, new coursemates, new subjects, new teachers—there was so much to discuss and wonder about. The streets felt long but fell short of the length of their conversations. Rounds of the campus brought them closer and made them fonder of each other.

The boy cracked a silly joke, the kind that no one ever laughs at. Yet the girl burst into laughter, causing the boy to shed tears of joy.

"This is my comfort; this is my world. I've finally found my new home," the boy thought to himself.

The girl was happy; her gregarious self had come out of hiding after years.

"Oh, I am late for the project meeting. I gotta run," she said.

The boy accompanied her to her hostel door, extracting every additional second of companionship possible.

"Come on, dude, you should show up for your group meeting too; you're late," the unwilling voice whispered to the boy.

3
Study Buddy

"You both are still asleep?!" exclaimed Harsha, seeing Sameer and his roommate Sid fast asleep at 8:45 a.m., just 15 minutes before their class was set to start at 9:00.

The lazy duo responded, "There are still 15 minutes to go."

Harsha was amazed by their casual attitude toward time.

"Gosh! The Prof. won't let you in after 9:00; wake up and get going!" she nudged them harder.

Reluctantly, the sleepy pair woke up, grabbed their books, and zoomed straight to the classroom, arriving just in time. Harsha became their friendly daily timekeeper and human alarm. If not for her, both of them would have ended up missing their mandatory attendance targets for the semester.

Looking back, I wonder how much self-discipline and the spirit of helping others were on glorious display in Harsha's daily actions. She was truly an individual of strong self-management and work ethic.

Two months later, it was time for semester exams. Harsha walked into their room and found them asleep. "It's

8:00 p.m., folks; dinner time. Shall we go? Have you completed your preparation for your exam tomorrow?" she asked.

To her surprise, the lazy roommates had yet to even start studying. After some prodding, they finally woke up, and the trio headed out to the cafeteria for dinner.

"What do we need to study for tomorrow, Harsha?" asked Sid calmly.

"Are you serious, Sid?" exclaimed Harsha, utterly disbelief at their level of unpreparedness. As she began to outline the syllabus, the roommates started to show signs of worry.

"That's quite a lot to read now; is there a shortcut?" asked Sameer.

"Oh boy! You must be kidding!" Harsha said, half-amused.

Concerned for her two friends, she offered to help them with their preparation by reading out the important learning summaries for each topic.

"Yeah, that sounds good," said Sameer happily as he began digging into his plate, momentarily setting aside his worries.

Right after dinner, Harsha took the boys back to their room, opened her books, and narrated a short summary for each of the four chapters that would be on the exam the next day.

Soon, these summary sessions before each exam gained popularity in the hostel. More and more boys lined up in the room, eager to hear her condensed learning points for each topic.

Harsha was their savior, a true study buddy.

4

Journey to Self

At the start of the new semester, the students walked up to the Academic Office to collect their new books. Curious to uncover the subjects for the semester, they opened their packs.

"Journey to Self! Wow, there's a subject with this title?!" exclaimed Sid.

Harsha read through the course contents and shared her thoughts with wonder.

"I wonder what we're going to uncover about ourselves through this subject," she said.

"I'm OK, You're OK is the prescribed book for this course. It's included in this pack," Sameer added.

The course was unique compared to any academic experience they had ever encountered.

Prof. Kalra showed up the very next day, introducing himself as the professor for this course. Some students described him as a highly experienced professor with deep expertise in psychology, while others felt uncomfortable with his teaching style, as delving into one's own self was an unsettling journey for many.

"This course sounds very exciting. We'll explore our life experiences to peel back the layers of our selves and reveal our core," Sameer shared.

"That's true, but we're supposed to write our own detailed autobiography up to this point. I don't hold my memories of the past so clearly; I might struggle with this," Harsha mentioned.

"We're so different in this regard. I have a vivid recollection of my past, yet I struggle to remember the information I need for exams. You, on the other hand, are great at recalling exam answers word for word but find it difficult to remember past experiences," Sameer said.

Sid, who was similar to Sameer in this aspect, added, "I also have clear, vivid memories of my past experiences, but I struggle to retain exam answers for long."

"That's why you both are roommates and very closely bonded. Birds of same feather flock together," Harsha suggested.

This made Harsha reflect on how different she was from Sameer. "What might explain our growing friendship when we are so different?" she thought to herself.

Sameer responded almost instantly, as if he had read her mind. Looking at Harsha with a hesitant smile, he said, "Opposites attract."

The two smiled and exchanged goodbyes. It was time to return to their hostels.

5

Sharing Their Past — Sid looks quieter today!

The assignment in the "Journey to Self" course, which involved documenting one's most impressionable moments, left many students with reflective emotions. The course also included a series of self-revealing psychometric assessments that provided deep personal insights. While some students dismissed the results and expressed discomfort with the methodology, many others valued the course for the profound self-awareness that emerged as a by-product.

The course prompted participants to relive some of their painful memories as well, causing past pain to resurface.

"Sid has been very quiet since yesterday; did he mention anything to you?" Harsha asked Sameer during their evening walk on campus.

"Oh really! As his roommate, I haven't noticed, but you did. That's impressive empathy," Sameer replied.

"See if you can talk to him," Harsha suggested.

"Of course, I will; I'll talk to him tonight. That's our favorite time to discuss life's philosophical topics," Sameer added.

"Sid, are you okay?" Sameer asked at midnight, noticing Sid's reflective demeanor.

"Yeah, Phaaji, I'm okay. I was thinking about a few instances I've written about in my autobiographical assignment," Sid replied.

The two had developed a brotherly bond, and Sid referred to Sameer as 'Phaaji,' a colloquial term for an elder brother.

"Want to go for coffee?" Sameer offered.

The two walked to the Nescafe, reflecting on their personal journeys.

"Sid, it's okay if you want to keep your deep past experiences to yourself; I won't ask. But know that if you feel like sharing, I'm here for you, brother," Sameer said.

Over a cup of coffee, Sid began to recount the most painful and life-altering incident from his life: the sudden loss of his dad five years ago.

Until that moment, Sameer had always felt that his own challenges and failures were significant in comparison. However, as he listened to Sid narrate the depth of his pain, Sameer was deeply moved and couldn't hold back his tears.

The pain, the loss, and the tragedy of losing someone in one's innermost circle were experiences Sameer had only heard about in stories but had never faced personally. It was a heart-wrenching and emotional account that strengthened the bond between the two friends.

"For what you have achieved despite this immense loss, it's truly commendable, Sid. I'm awestruck by your resilience and the way you've found your direction despite losing the lighthouse of your life at such a critical time," Sameer said as he hugged his younger brother from another mother.

6

Harsha's Story

"I spoke to Sid; my story and challenges are nothing compared to his," Sameer shared with Harsha the next day. She was moved listening to his story as well and shed a tear.

"How has your story been?" asked Sameer.

"As I said, my childhood memories are not vivid. All I remember is my sister, who is more like a twin to me since the age gap is just over a year," Harsha narrated.

She continued sharing some adorable childhood moments with her younger sister, Jaya.

"Our parents worked, so we were looked after by our grandmother. I recall how she would make sweet kuttis for us. I also remember how our dad would make us sit next to each other and affectionately feed us both," Harsha shared, smiling.

She recounted how she and her sister, Jaya, would get caught sneaking into their uncle's room late at night while his family was busy watching movies on TV. She described her ten-years-younger brother, Sachin, as a joy to have around.

"At 10 years old, Jaya and I would actively babysit our brother, play with him, change his diapers, and feed him until our mom returned from the office," she added.

Once she started, she had many more beautiful moments to share, from dance classes to twinning with her sister. She reminisced about the few special vacations their family took to hill stations.

"My Nanaji (maternal grandfather) and dad are two big influences in my life," Harsha shared.

She continued to express her admiration for these two gentlemen and the impact they had on her. She shared inspiring tales of her grandfather, Nanaji, from his freedom-fighting days to his editorial career.

She recalled special moments of visiting her grandparents in Mumbai during summer breaks and being treated to love-filled Sindhi delicacies. "I was taught by my mother, who had a demanding full-time job. She would also need to cook in the evenings for the family, balancing her tasks by helping me with my homework at the same time," Harsha shared with inspiration in her eyes.

After exchanging beautiful memories from her childhood, Harsha spoke about some tough phases of her life.

"I remember how difficult it was for us to move out of our joint family home to our nuclear home and how my parents faced challenges during that critical time," Harsha reminisced.

"The toughest part was when my dad came to Mumbai to drop me off at college. After settling me in at my grandparents' home, he turned and left for Delhi. I thought to myself, that's it? He is gone? I am now left to fend for myself?" Harsha shared, her voice cracking.

"Life in Mumbai was tough, and it took me a long time to feel settled. From carrying heavy grocery bags back home to arranging my meals by myself to traveling on local buses and figuring it all out alone, the list went on," she continued, sharing her remarkable learning experiences during her college years.

There was something the two understood deeply about each other. Their challenges sounded similar: experiences of loneliness, self-responsibility, abandonment, and homesickness.

She also explained how these tough experiences made her more confident and self-reliant. There were plenty of happy and adventurous tales from her college life as well, which brought laughter to their conversation.

The stories continued as the sun set behind a beautiful line of trees in the background of Nescafe.

7
Sameer's Mixed Bag

Listening to the two friends' tales, Sameer felt that his challenges were belittled. He had a relatively perfect upbringing, with hardly any changes until his schooling. It was after his schooling that he became disappointed with the quality of options he had created for himself for graduation.

He shared how one year of underperformance in 12th grade downgraded his future options, despite having a strong academic record up until then.

He felt disappointed that, when it mattered most, he could not perform to his potential. He had lived with this regret until he finally felt good about gaining admission to this prestigious institute for his post-graduation.

Sameer also spoke about coping with loneliness and sadness due to the lack of deep connections with those around him. He expressed despair at failing to find and nurture any romantic relationships in his life.

"I am the only one in my family pursuing a career in the private sector. Most of my relatives are in government jobs. But I want to be in business; that's what my ancestors did, and I feel that this entrepreneurial spirit lies dormant in my DNA. I want to ignite it and establish a business after a few years of working in corporate companies," he narrated passionately.

He also discussed how an abrupt division in his family affected him, as his separation from his grandparents left him feeling depressed and lost. At the crucial time of taking entrance examinations for postgraduate courses, he could not give the necessary attention to his grandparents. He had been living with that guilt as well.

Nevertheless, Sameer was thrilled about his prospects now and had clarity about the future.

"I want to be a trainer, and this post-graduation in HR will help me become a good one," he shared with clarity and confidence.

Harsha empathized with Sameer as he shared his story and felt blessed to finally have friends who were close enough to listen and understand.

"Thanks for listening to me," said Sameer.

"Your story sounds great, but if you wish to earn better marks on this assignment, you should consider adding some spicy incidents too," grinned Harsha.

8

Veer Zaara — The First Kiss!

"There's this new movie in theaters that is garnering great feedback. It's an amazing love story about an Indian Air Force officer and a girl from across the border," the boy says.

"Veer Zaara, right? Yes, I know about it," the girl responds.

"Shall we go? Would you be interested?" the boy asks.

"Sure, in the evening after classes?" the girl replies.

"Yes, shall I check with Sid, Kunal, and anyone else if they would like to join?" the boy continues, and the girl affirms.

After classes, the two meet.

"What's the plan?" the girl asks.

"Both Sid and Kunal are scheduled to attend the industry speaker session today, so they cannot join," the boy explains.

"Even Bhawna is scheduled for the same; she can't join either. I asked her," the girl says.

"So, what do we do? Do you still want to go?" the boy asks.

"Yes, let's go. Tomorrow, we have our scheduled duty, and then the weekend will be with our families. So, shall we go today?" the girl responds.

The two decide to go to the movie. After a short break, they text each other and meet in the parking lot. The boy takes out his scooter, and the two ride off to the theater.

"Veer-Zaara" is a timeless saga of love, sacrifice, and destiny that transcends borders. Veer, an Indian Air Force officer, and Zaara, a Pakistani woman from an influential family, fall deeply in love, only to be torn apart by fate and societal barriers. Their love endures through years of separation, silent longing, and selfless sacrifices, proving that true love knows no boundaries. With soulful melodies, heart-wrenching moments, and a love that stands the test of time, *Veer-Zaara* is a poetic ode to the kind of love that waits—forever.

The theatre is half empty. During one engrossing, heart-wrenching scene, the two hold each other's hands. They immerse themselves deeply in the romantic movie, sharing a common interest in the genre.

The depth of the scenes blurs the lines between the act and reality. Their hearts warm to each other as the boy gazes at the girl. He leans in an inch closer as she closes her eyes in loving acceptance. They kiss with trembling lips and bated breath. Time stands still in that moment— their first kiss.

As they come to their senses, a surge of joy and guilt washes over them. They withdraw and feel awkward about what just happened. Unable to look at each other for the next few minutes, they freeze, still holding hands but not moving at all.

The conflicting emotions of ecstasy from the kiss and the guilt of having kissed numb their thoughts. The movie no longer makes any sense to either of them.

A few moments later, as if their minds are processing in sync, they look at each other again and kiss. They are happy but also scared about what they have just done again. The first kiss is special for both, making them reflective.

The two silently exit the theatre after the half-watched movie, unable to meet each other's gaze—excited in their hearts but pensive in their thoughts. They quietly ride back to the hostel.

"How am I going to even face her once we reach the hostel?" the boy thinks.

"My first kiss—wow, this was special. Is it real? But it feels awkward," the girl thinks.

The boy rides slowly back into the parking lot. They get out, shy about looking at each other, and walk back to the hostel block in silence.

"I don't have the words to describe what happened. Shall we just go back to normal and I'll ensure we maintain our boundaries from now on?" the boy blurts out, feeling pressured to break the awkward silence.

"Yeah, let's keep things as they were and try to feel normal," the girl responds, also feeling the pressure to say something.

The two turn to their respective blocks, walking away with joyful smiles and a sense of disbelief about what had just happened. The experience of their first kiss will take time to settle into their hearts.

9

Love is in the Air!

The next morning, the boy wakes up a little nervous. He hasn't had much sleep, constantly thinking about the first kiss and still in disbelief.

The girl hesitates before coming in to wake the roommates, unsure of the appropriateness of any messages that might be passed on to the boy through her actions. She has been reflecting on the kiss all night as well.

Deciding to overcome the awkwardness, she steps into room #126.

"Oh hi, you're already awake?!" she asks, seeing the boy up and ready.

"Hey, hi... yes, I got up on time today. How are you?" the boy replies pensively.

After exchanging some formal pleasantries, the two walk together to class. Sid follows them later. It's a long day filled with classes and an evening industry speaker session. They finally return to their hostels late in the evening.

"Shall we meet for dinner in the cafeteria?" texts the boy.

"Yes, sure, see you in 10 minutes," responds the girl.

Over dinner, a few other friends join in, and the casual banter eases the tension between the two. As dinner ends, the boy second-guesses asking the girl for a walk on campus. They have developed a habit of these late-night post-dinner strolls, but today the boy seems a bit hesitant to ask.

"Walk?" the girl inquires.

The boy, relieved and hiding his smile, replies, "Sure!"

The two try to behave normally and open up the same safe topics for conversation.

After a long walk, they warm up as the boy tells a joke that makes the girl laugh. After five rounds of walk in the campus, they take a break by sitting on their favorite bench, secluded at the end of the street, flanked by tall, towering trees.

Moments later, as luck would have it, the power goes out, and the streetlights turn off. Their hearts warm, and they feel an irresistible fire swelling within them as they share a passionate kiss.

This time, the moment feels more accepting, made special by the heavenly gods who keep the lights off for an extended period. They pause when reality kicks in about what just happened. Turning away for a moment, they look back and kiss again. The streetlight remains off, and the intoxicating smell of jasmine flowers fills the air.

Love is in the air!

10

Passion and Projects!

What ensued over the next few days was a whirlwind of passion and projects. The two would secretly steal moments together amidst the busy campus life, sometimes holding hands in the library while browsing through books for cases, and occasionally staying behind in class to catch a private moment after everyone else had left.

Evening strolls to the on-campus Nescafe often sparked deep, jovial conversations, as their hearts longed to share everything with each other. Their space was becoming deeply personal, special, and safe from judgment.

The two friends were slowly becoming each other's trusted confidants. Midnight scooter rides to roadside eateries under the trees nearby added to their shared adventures.

Their ability to work together seamlessly, despite their opposite personalities, was uncanny. They began selecting the same project teams whenever possible, and their teamwork started to yield impressive results.

The girl's passion and energy to perform well inspired the boy to bring out his best in various assignments and projects. A partnership that would last a lifetime was being forged, as if heavenly angels were looking down upon them, smiling at their handiwork.

"Look at this!" the boy pointed to a colorful notice on the board about a B-School competition.

"The prize money is decent. It could add to some pocket money," he said.

"We're in our first year, and second-year students will also be competing. Do you think it's worth it?" asked the girl.

"There's nothing to lose and a lot to learn—and enjoy—by working together on this. What do you say?" he encouraged.

"Sure, let's do it," the girl replied, feeling motivated.

"But why are you focused on the prize money?" she asked.

"I worked for four years before joining this full time course. I am used to the financial independence of earning my own money. I feel awkward about the thought of becoming dependent on my parents again, especially since my savings will soon run dry," the boy explained.

"It's okay; they are your parents, and this dependence is temporary—just for two years," the girl said to comfort him.

"Yes, that's true; however, there's no harm in trying to earn some extra cash through these prizes, is there?" the boy added, which made the girl determined to excel for their team of two.

The two worked very hard over the next week, crafting their solution for the complex case study competition. It was an immense learning experience, and they seemed to enjoy their newfound passion for both their love and their work. They made it to the finals of the presentation but didn't win the coveted prize.

However, the results were still gratifying for both, as they celebrated their first project together with a discreet kiss over coffee at Nescafe.

23

11

The Proposal to an Uncertain Future!

By now, the two had been spotted a couple of times by their classmates, who noticed how close they had grown. They became the silent topic of conversation on campus. Both started facing the obvious question from friends all around: "Are you two going out?"

After reflecting on their current reality, they reached a point where the obvious needed to be addressed. During one such late-night stroll around campus after dinner, the boy brought up the topic. "Friends have started talking about us. They think we're dating," he stated.

"Yes, I wasn't prepared for such questions and the attention. I don't know how to respond or what to say," the girl replied, looking confused.

"How do we want this to look for us in the future?" the boy asked.

The girl flipped the question back to him.

"This is the very first time I've grown so fond of someone and come so close to you. I'm a long-term commitment guy; if I'm in, I'm in for the long haul. What do you think?" he shared.

"I adore being with you. I think of us all the time. We come from different backgrounds and religions, so I'm uncertain if I'll get my parents' permission for a long-term commitment when the time comes," the girl expressed her willingness along with her apprehensions.

"My parents also belong to different religions, and I believe they will understand and support us when we explain our situation to them in the future," the boy replied.

"I feel uncertain about my parents' support and approval, but if you stand by me during those times, I will try to convince them with all my heart," the girl said with determination.

"I don't know what the outcome of convincing our parents will be in the future. But whenever we reach that stage, after our course and once we start our careers, I will be there with you till the very end. I promise to be your equal partner in this life's journey as well. Will we win our coveted prize then? That's in the hands of the Almighty," the boy added.

The two shared a hug, looked at each other, and smiled with moist eyes. "Cheers to our commitment to an uncertain future," they said in unison as they clinked their water cups.

Friends joined in, interrupting the conversation. Amidst the group chatter and banter, the two kept locking eyes with each other, feeling the incompleteness of their conversation.

There was something amiss, and the girl's phone chimed with an incoming message. The boy looked at her with bated breath as she unlocked her phone to check the message.

"I love you..." read the message from him.

The girl texted back with a love-filled smile, "I love you too!"

12

We are in love!

The time that followed was filled with sunshine and rainbows, poems and couplets, hugs and gifts, as if the two were finally living an experience they had yearned for so long. Their friends had figured out by now that the two were a couple, and there were friendly comments and banter all around.

Life seemed more purposeful, and their ambitions soared high as the new couple in town went about sharing their dreams. They spent most of their time together, and despite being in the same class, if they had to sit apart, they missed even those little moments without each other. Their bond was growing deeper and stronger. They cared for one another and had developed some wonderful common friendship groups on campus.

The monthly campus parties were even more fun now. They would dance together late into the night after working hard through the day. They ventured out to see every new movie in theaters and looked forward to exciting midnight scooter rides to explore new food shacks in town.

Birthdays became the most special celebrations for them, one after the other. The two tried to make each occasion memorable for the other on consecutive birthdays.

The boy sometimes imagined, What if eventually one of us is left alone? How would the birthdays feel then without a partner? The thought would cross his mind, but he would rationalize himself back into reality to enjoy the current moment.

They got creative with nicknaming each other, using terms like Babes, Bebo, Bobo, and more. All these adorable, cute names were texted back and forth. There was love all around, a spring in every step, warmth in every hug, and passion in every kiss.

13

We Love Babies

Those were the days of email forwards. The two would often share interesting forwards with one another and eagerly await each other's reactions.

One such forward from the girl read, "Hey Bobo, look at these cute kids' pictures in this email. I want our kids to be just as cute." The email contained images of adorable babies that lit up the boy's heart.

They had just discovered their shared fascination for babies. Both adored looking at cute baby pictures, marking yet another unique and common interest between them.

They were always on the lookout for forwards featuring cute little baby pictures to send to each other.

Their discussions often revolved around kids and how many they would want to have. "I want three cute and adorable children, just like you," the boy would always say.

"Do you know what it takes to raise children? Two is fine," the girl would insist in response.

"My cousin has a toddler, and she lives nearby now. I'm visiting her to see them; do you want to come?" asked the boy.

"I want to come, but what will you say to her? Will you tell her that this girl from your class has come to see her child?" the girl inquired.

"My cousin sister Chitra is more like a real sister to me. She will understand what's happening between us, even if nothing is said. Let's go! And she is a great cook," the boy enticed.

They were now ready to go, especially since a delicious home-cooked meal was part of the deal. Chitra was the first from Sameer's family to meet Harsha and immediately sensed the spark between them without a word being spoken.

The acceptance was instant and heartfelt. The playful toddler added cheer to the evening. The warm, tasty homely food made the atmosphere even more delightful.

The two lovers cherished the idea of a cozy home with a lovely child around—an idea to hold onto for a long time and an evening to remember forever!

14
The Equation of Us

She tapped her fingers against the edge of her coffee mug, staring at the steam rising from it like a fading ghost of her patience. Across the café table, He shifted uncomfortably, his jaw tight, his own cup untouched.

Their first fight.

Neither had expected it. Not this soon, at least.

It had started as something silly—an argument about a group project. Harsha, an ambitious organized student, believed that everything should be well-planned, structured, and submitted early. Sameer, a laid-back yet highly creative student, thrived on last-minute pressure, confident that "great ideas need space to breathe."

The conversation had started as a debate, turned into a disagreement, and then, somewhere along the way, a battle of principles.

"You can't just assume everything will work out at the last minute!" Harsha snapped.

"And you can't plan creativity into a fixed schedule!" Sameer countered.

The irritation lingered, stretching between them like an invisible barrier.

Now, sitting in their favorite campus café, they had fallen into a tense silence.

Harsha glanced at Sameer's face—normally so warm, full of mischief. Today, it was distant, unreadable.

"Are we really going to sit here and sulk?" she finally asked, forcing a calm tone.

Sameer exhaled sharply. "I don't know, Harsha. I mean, do you really think I'm irresponsible?"

Harsha hesitated. "No. I know you're smart, but..." She sighed, running a hand through her hair. "I just— I like stability. Structure. It makes me feel safe."

Sameer looked up at that, his features softening. "And I like flexibility because it makes me feel free."

Harsha blinked. She had never thought of it that way. She saw last-minute work as laziness, but to him, it was a method of inspiration.

Sameer hesitated before continuing, "Look, I get it. You like to be prepared, and I like to trust the process. But I don't want to fight over something like this. We're different, but isn't that a good thing? I have always been misjudged for my last minute actions to be laziness"

Harsha looked at him—really looked at him. He wasn't just defending his point. He was reaching out, trying to bridge the gap between them.

A slow smile formed on her lips. "Okay. I am sorry"

Sameer replied. "Ok. I am sorry too."

She nodded. "We are good?"

He held up his coffee mug. "To our first fight?"

Harsha smiled, clinking her cup against his. "To learning how to fight better."

And just like that, the first storm had passed.

Because love wasn't about winning arguments—it was about understanding the person sitting across from you, even when you disagreed.

15

Meeting is Joy, Parting is Sorrow!

It was time for a two-month internship during the course. All the companies had visited the campus over the past few months to select students for internships, and the two of them were selected by different companies in different cities.

On one hand, there was joy in embarking on a new career experience; on the other hand, there was the unsettling feeling of being apart for two months. As fate would have it, both were assigned training-based internship projects in their respective organizations.

"I have always envisioned a career as a trainer and specifically requested a training project during my interview. It's such a coincidence that you were also assigned a training project for your internship," Sameer wondered.

"Yeah, it's a pleasant surprise to receive a project in the same field. I was open to any project, as I neither have preferences nor any past experience like yours in training," Harsha responded.

"Could be a divine hint," the boy said with an enchanting smile.

"But I am going to miss you so much," he shared, wrapping his arms around his beloved.

"I don't know how I will get through this time without you," she expressed.

"Meeting is joy, parting is sorrow; the time will fly, and we shall meet tomorrow," he recited poetically.

The year came to a close, and the students packed up their belongings.

It was time to head to different cities, different companies, and tackle different projects during their internships. There was excitement and anxiety about this new chapter. The adventure was on the horizon, but there was also separation anxiety, especially for the two of them.

Over the next eight weeks, the distance could not dim their love; on the contrary, their bond grew stronger.

Throughout each day, they exchanged text messages and longed for detailed phone calls in the evenings. Love, work, and baby pictures were common themes in their conversations.

The day of their return was special. Both had butterflies in their stomachs about reuniting after this long eight-week gap, which felt like ages.

They were eager to give each other gifts they had purchased with their stipends. The excitement and nervousness thrilled them as they chose to meet at Nescafe.

The boy rushed to Nescafe and saw the girl already waiting there. Their steps slowed as they looked at each other. Their eyes sparkled with joy, and their hearts finally found comfort in being together again.

"Didn't I say, meeting is joy, parting is sorrow; the time will fly, and we shall meet tomorrow?" said the boy.

"The time has flown by, and now that we are together, it feels pure joy," the girl replied with a smile.

A warm hug and coffee marked the start of their second year of campus life.

16
The Night of Fate and Free Will

The clock struck midnight, but neither Sid nor Sam had any intention of sleeping. Their dorm room, cluttered with books, half-eaten snacks, and an old lava lamp casting flickering shadows, had turned into a philosophical battleground.

Sid, leaning back against his pillow, tossed a peanut in the air and caught it. "Listen, Phaaji, everything that happens—our successes, failures, even this conversation—is pre-destined. We're just playing out what's already been written."

Sam scoffed, sitting cross-legged on his chair. "Oh, come on. That's the laziest way to look at life. If everything is pre-decided, why do we even try? We make our own choices, and those choices shape our future."

Sid smirked. "You think you're choosing, but you're just following a path designed for you. Think about it—why did you pick this post graduate course? Because of your dad's influence? Your environment? Your natural inclination? You never actually *chose* it. It was always meant to be."

Sam rubbed his temples, refusing to surrender. "That doesn't make sense. I could've chosen Art if I wanted to. The fact that I weighed my options means I had a choice. Every decision we make pushes life in a different direction. We are the architects of our own destiny."

Sid chuckled. "Architects? More like actors reading from a script we didn't write. Why do some people succeed against all odds while others fail despite working hard? If destiny didn't exist, why is life so unfair?"

Sam threw a pillow at him. "That's because people who succeed make different choices! Hard work, smart decisions, persistence—these are the things that change fate."

Sid caught the pillow and grinned. "Or maybe they were *meant* to make those choices. Ever thought of that?"

The debate raged on, weaving through religion, science, personal experiences, and stories of fate-defying underdogs. They argued over Einstein, Gita and butterfly effects, each throwing facts, logic, and random internet theories at each other.

At 5 AM, their voices were hoarse, their minds exhausted. Sid lay sprawled on his bed, Sam slumped in his chair and said "Shall we go out for coffee and breakfast? Need to rush to the class as there is no time to sleep now"

On their way back from an extended discussion over coffee and breakfast, Sid asked sleepily "So?"

Sam sighed, rubbing his eyes. "I still think we create our own path."

Sid smirked. "And I still think we're just following it."

A long silence.

Then, a laugh.

Neither had won, but neither had lost.

Outside, the sun began to rise, as if *destined* to, yet completely by *its own will*.

39

17

The first prized cheque

It was the season of Inter B-School competitions, and all of them featured decent prize money.

With the stipend earned during his internship, Sameer could self-fund his expenses for the next few months. The prospect of winning some cash to cover his expenses was very enticing.

"Harsha, look at this! Five grand for the winning team. We can participate individually or in teams of two. Shall we register for this one?" Sameer asked his favorite partner on campus, pointing at the announcement on the notice board.

"There are two rounds. If our paper gets shortlisted in the first round, we will be called to present in front of the panel in the final round," Harsha read aloud.

"Okay, let's do it," Harsha replied, getting excited too.

In the days that followed, the two stretched a lot in the evenings after classes to write their paper for submission to the competition. They would sit in each other's rooms for long periods, researching, discussing, debating, and composing their paper.

After collaborative discussions, Sameer would typically sit in a chair with his legs propped on the bed, narrating the text for the paper while gazing at the ceiling. Harsha would usually type the text on the computer as she diligently listened to his narrative and added her points wherever appropriate.

For references, they would visit the library, browse through various titles, and select relevant sections to strengthen their paper.

After a week of effort, the paper was finally looking complete.

"That's it, Sam! Let's submit it now. We have just one hour left before the deadline to send the paper via email," insisted Harsha.

Sameer continued to add last-minute ideas and edits. "Done! Hit send. Five minutes left," Harsha exclaimed as he finally sent the email just in time before the deadline.

The two hugged each other in celebration, even though this was just the initial submission. The experience of completing the paper together after a week of effort was immensely gratifying. Following this experience, they began to keep a vigilant eye on any new B-School competition announcements that appeared on the notice board.

A few days later, Sameer rushed to Harsha's room in excitement. "Check your email!" he shouted as she quickly booted up her desktop computer, anticipating some encouraging news.

"Did we really make it?" she asked even before the suspense was revealed in the email. "Ahh, I knew you would guess it," Sameer laughed in sheer joy.

"Yay! We made it!" The two danced with glee, jumping on the bed.

They were charged up to give their best in the final round as well. The presentation took place on the campus of the organizing B-School, a well-known institution near Harsha's parents' home.

"Our presentation will be over by 12 PM, and since my home is nearby, my mom has invited us for lunch. Will you come?" asked Harsha.

"Yes, surely!" replied Sameer, feeling a flutter of anxious butterflies in his stomach.

On one hand, he was eager to see Harsha's family and her home; on the other, he was anxious that if he didn't get accepted a few months later, it would break his heart.

It was the day of redemption. The two, dressed in their formal best, rode in an auto rickshaw to the venue. They had rehearsed their slides countless times and their confidence was high. However, during the panel's question round, Sameer got nervous and blurted out an incomplete response. Harsha quickly filled in and elaborated, making their answer sound complete.

The competition was stiff, as there were teams from several top B-Schools in the finals. When the results were announced, they found out they were runners-up. They were overjoyed; their first joint project had achieved success, and the cash prize for the runners-up team sweetened the deal.

Excitedly, the two rode in an autorickshaw to Harsha's home, with Sameer anxiously waiting behind her as she joyfully rang the doorbell.

Her loving and gentle mother opened the door, and Harsha hugged her in excitement. "We won the second prize, Mom!" "Wow, congratulations to the two of you!" her mother exclaimed, expressing her joy as she met Sameer for the very first time.

A bit shy, conscious, and happy, Sameer entered their beautiful, cozy home, where her mother made him feel comfortable. The first thing he noticed was the picture of divine Guruji Nanak adorning the wall.

He bowed to the photo and asked Harsha quietly, "I didn't know you followed Guru Nanak Dev ji. I feel a strong connection to Him."

"Yes, even as Sindhis, we follow the teachings of Guru Nanak Dev ji. Our Naaniji taught us the first few stanzas of the Gurbani when we were little," Harsha explained.

It was another shared experience for the two of them, both having learned the same stanza from their respective grandmothers.

Harsha's mother's homemade lunch was delicious and full of love. "Aunty, I really love this kebab sabzi. Thank you; you've made it so well," Sameer shared his appreciation while enjoying the meal.

After relishing the meal and a warm afternoon in the home where they would later create countless memories together, Sameer left in the autorickshaw, looking up at the first-floor balcony where his dearest Harsha was smiling and waving at him all the way down the street, until the auto turned, and he could no longer be seen.

18
The Fall of Guilt

Thursday evenings had a light schedule, as the classes ended earlier. The two often ventured out on those evenings to nearby malls and movies. One such Thursday, they set out to watch a movie at the theater.

Sameer took out his scooter, and they drove away. Midway through the journey, it began to drizzle, and the streetlights in the lonely bylanes of the city were out. In the dark, they chatted as they drove.

"Should we turn back? It's started to drizzle," Sameer asked.

"I don't know; maybe it will settle down in a bit," replied Harsha.

"Okay! Let's try riding for another mile or two and reassess then," he said.

"Thud, boom, screech." The scooter hit an unexpected speed-breaker, landing in a water-filled pothole with a thud as Sameer momentarily lost his balance.

As he regained his composure, panic set in when he saw Harsha fall off the scooter. The image of Harsha lying on the road in shock and bleeding from the face still sends chills down his spine to this day.

He rushed to help her up and panicked at the sight of her torn top, ruffled bleeding face, and shocked expression.

He cried out in bewilderment, feeling lost on that deserted stretch of road. He pulled her to the side and helped her sit on the pavement while he searched for water in the scooter's basket. He found a water bottle and grabbed his handkerchief. Gently, he cleaned her bruises, checking with her to gauge the extent of her injuries.

She appeared to be in shock but managed to get up and sit back on the scooter with his support. Knowing of a hospital nearby, he decided to rush there.

"Sid, we've had an accident; please rush to Anand Hospital. I'm fine, but Harsha is hurt. We're on our way. Please inform Kunal as well, and you two come immediately," he told Sid over the phone, his voice filled with distress.

"There are two stitches required, one above her upper lip and another on her elbow. She seems to be in shock. We'll need to wait and monitor her for some time before we assess further. We need permission from a family member before proceeding," the emergency department doctor informed them.

"Sameer, I've spoken to Harsha's dad, and he's on his way. He would like to speak with you," Bhawna, a mutual friend who had rushed to the hospital upon hearing the news, informed him. By now, many of their classmates had arrived at the hospital in support after the news spread throughout the group.

Sameer spoke to Harsha's dad for the first time during this catastrophic situation. He had never imagined that this would be the way he would get introduced to her dad. The calm and understanding voice of the gentleman on the other side of the phone said, "Okay, please ask the doctor to do what needs to be done, as I am on my way to the hospital."

The burden of guilt and the anguish of seeing his beloved bleed in front of him were too heavy as he broke down, crying on Sid's shoulders.

"Please, sir, kindly confirm, double confirm, and reconfirm that there will be no mark from your stitch whatsoever on the area above her lips," Sameer screamed multiple times at the attending doctor. The doctor was confident that the stitch was small and that its mark would fade with time.

He called his father and confided in him about what had just happened. His father quickly consulted a dermatologist friend and explained the situation to him. The renowned dermatologist assured him that this type of stitch typically should not leave any mark in the future. He promised that once the stitch was done, he would personally come to assess the situation and provide some creams to address the concern.

Harsha's dad and sister arrived at the hospital amidst the crowd of classmates who had gathered. Sameer anxiously recounted the whole incident to Harsha's dad, a calm and understanding gentleman.

Harsha received treatment, though she still appeared to be in shock. Seeing her, Sameer was overwhelmed with guilt and pain.

"We will need to admit her overnight to monitor her condition. We will perform some tests in the morning to rule out any internal injury before we are convinced about discharging her," the treating doctor informed him.

Harsha's sister offered to stay with her overnight as her attendant. Her dad left the hospital after she was moved to the room. The friends returned to campus sometime later, and Sameer sat on a bench in the emergency ward near Harsha's room.

He could not move for hours, still reeling from the shock of what had just happened and weighed down by the guilt from her fall.

This turned out to be his longest night as he sat anxiously on that bench, consumed by fear, pain, and more guilt over the possibility of any internal injury. The scene of the tragic fall kept replaying in his mind, causing him further distress throughout the night.

He kept visiting her room, peeking in to check with her sister if all was okay. Harsha was asleep under the effects of the medication, and her vitals seemed fine.

Jaya, Harsha's younger sister by a year, who resembled her more like a twin, grew suspicious about Sameer and Harsha's relationship, noticing his concern throughout the night.

At 7 a.m., Jaya stepped out of the room and informed Sameer, "She just woke up and asked for you." Sameer hurried in, teary-eyed, and walked up to her as she lifted her hand to be held. He took her hand, trying to hold back his tears. Before he could ask her anything, she asked, "How are you? Did you get hurt too?"

He apologized for causing her pain as she assured him that she was fine and had simply lost her balance on the bump.

"I'll be here until you're discharged today," Sameer promised.

"You shouldn't miss your classes today. Jaya is here, and my dad will be here soon," she replied.

"I want to stay here until your discharge," he insisted.

"Bhawna, can you please keep the notes from today's class for me and Harsha?" Sameer asked Bhawna over the phone.

"Yeah, sure, Sameer. By the way, Harsha's dad was asking if you and Harsha are dating. He seems to think so. I told him you're just friends, but he didn't seem convinced. I thought I should let you know," Bhawna said.

Meanwhile, Sameer's dad called for an update on Harsha. Sameer informed him of her status and added, "Papa, I wanted to let you know that I'm still at the hospital and missing my classes today. I'll be here until her discharge. She's very special to me." His dad understood their relationship.

Later in the day, some additional medical tests came back normal, and Harsha was discharged. She left with her family in their car, and Sameer walked over to his scooter.

"Thanks, buddy, for being my wonderful partner for years. We've travelled a thousand miles together. But it's time to say goodbye now," Sameer said to his scooter as he vowed never to ride a two-wheeler again.

19

Forging Strong Partnerships for Life

The two-year postgraduate course was in its final leg, and Harsha and Sameer were gaining momentum in their group assignments and various B-School competitions.

By now, they could form their own project groups, and they had gravitated towards a group of close friends. Kunal had become a dear friend and buddy.

In project assignments, Kunal, Uma, Harsha, and Sameer often teamed up, boosting their team's overall score. The group was cohesive and worked well together, performing admirably in all their course presentations.

On the competition front, they quickly registered for every competition announced. They frequently made it past the initial rounds and reached the finals in a couple of events.

They travelled together to various B-Schools both within and outside the city, bringing home accolades along with some attractive cash rewards.

The most memorable wins were at IIM Lucknow and as National Winners of the L&T Built to Last Competition.

The latter was especially significant as it was a team effort by Harsha, Sid, and Sameer. The three spent four consecutive sleepless nights working every available minute on the submission for the national-level competition.

They were overjoyed when the results were announced and they received their accolades. For Sameer, the cash reward was a significant motivator, allowing him to feel financially independent for a few more months.

The experience also strengthened their confidence and trust in their partnership.

"I love working together," Harsha expressed.

"We should tackle bigger projects together sometime in life," Sameer added.

"Wouldn't it be fun if we could work together in the area we love the most and also earn from it?" Sameer wondered.

That day, the seeds of their desire to work together and earn a living from their passions were sown in their minds.

20
Sunrise in Goa!?

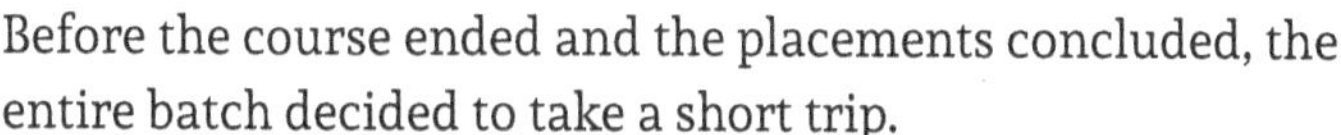

Before the course ended and the placements concluded, the entire batch decided to take a short trip.

Different groups made plans to various fun places like hill stations and beaches. A large majority of the batchmates planned a trip to Goa, a beautiful former Portuguese town and a popular beach destination in India.

"We are nine of us, right?" Sid asked Sam to double-confirm the headcount in their itinerary.

"Wait, add Ankit and Divya also. They just texted me," Sameer added.

"Okay, shall I do the final booking now for the 11 of us?" Sid insisted, as the train ticket portal was still showing available tickets.

They were at risk of losing out on confirmed tickets if there were any further delays.

"Gaurav is calling; wait," Sameer said.

"Fast, phaaji, fast. I am worried that the tickets may not remain available online for long," Sid replied anxiously.

"Gaurav has also confirmed. Let's add him in. We are all set now for 12 of us. Book it, bro," Sameer said excitedly.

After filling in all the details across multiple screens and railway booking accounts, Sid announced, "Yes, we are all booked and confirmed."

"Yay! We are confirmed now to go to Goa. Tickets done!" everyone cheered as the message reached them all.

"Where do we stay?" Harsha asked.

The two men looked at each other, completely clueless, and burst out laughing.

"It has taken us 10 days to finalize our ever-changing plan of dates and tickets to Goa. I'm scared to even think about how much effort it will take to find accommodation for all of us, considering everyone's preferences," Sid shared.

"Don't worry, dear; we will figure something out when we get there," Sameer assured, lacking a concrete plan.

"What confidence! I admire your belief in the unknown," Harsha laughed, prompting everyone to join in on the laughter. Everyone was just too happy and excited about having finalized the plan to visit Goa.

For most of them, this was their first-ever trip to Goa. There were hardly any options online to search for and book accommodation.

Through some contacts and connections, the group found a place to stay for the first night in a company guest house. The next day, the entire group scoured the city of Goa in search of accommodation.

"Wow! This one is just perfect," Amit said, trying to persuade the group to affirm their decision about this property, which they had stumbled upon after a long day of searching.

Everyone was tired and in no mood to look at any more properties, so they jumped right into this hotel.

After spending four days sightseeing in Goa as a group, the friends decided to spend their last evening at a beach shack over dinner and drinks. The evening felt so special that Sameer didn't want it to end.

Everyone called it a day by 1 a.m., but Sameer, Sid, and Harsha were so at peace with the setup that they wanted to stay a little longer.

They had never experienced the tranquil seaside at night, with the sea waves kissed by moonlight.

"It's the last order, Sir," said the waiter.

"I would like to enjoy two beers for as long as I can tonight. I don't want to leave this place. What will we do back at the hotel?" Sameer replied.

"Exactly! I also want to be here longer," said Sid.

"I'm with you, Bobo. Whatever you decide," Harsha said with blissful eyes as she sipped her first-ever Breezer.

"Cool then! Let others go, and we can stay here for as long as we want," announced Sameer.

"Can you bring us four beers and two Breezers as our last order for the night?" they asked the waiter.

"And I hope we can stay here for as long as we want with the candles lit," added Sameer.

"Yes, Sir. You can stay as long as you'd like. I will keep the candles lit on your table," offered the waiter.

The scene was perfect: the moon-kissed sea waves, the rhythmic sound of rising and falling waves, the calmness of the sea, and the depth of their conversations.

"Let's wait here to witness the sunrise. What do you say, folks?" Sameer proposed boldly.

His two companions agreed instantly, and their conversations continued.

The music in the shack played as Sid and Sameer delved deep into their discussion about destiny vs. free will.

"Phaaji, where is Harsha?" Sid panicked, noticing that Harsha was missing from her chair.

They were so engrossed in their talk that they failed to notice Harsha walk away.

They looked around and found Harsha running toward the sea.

"There she is. What is she doing running toward the sea?" Sameer exclaimed as the two rushed to catch up with her.

"Let me dance! And you should dance too," said the cheerful Harsha to her beloved.

The two danced to the sounds of nature while Sid danced solo at a distance with his beer.

"Looks like you drank a bit too much too quickly, Bebo," Sameer commented.

"Well, I don't know about that. What I know is that I'm happy, I want to dance, and I love you, Bobo," Harsha said ecstatically.

After a few dance moves, the three returned to their candlelit table. The conversations continued for a while before Harsha ran off to the sea again, causing panic once more.

The three enjoyed the night on the beach. They stayed through the wee hours and were now tired, but they wanted to linger a little longer to witness the sunrise.

"I'm tired, but now that we've spent so many hours here, I want to see the sunrise and then leave," Sid said.

"Yes, buddy, as we promised ourselves, we shall leave only after the sunrise," Sameer added, as Harsha lay comfortably asleep on two lounge chairs joined together on the beach.

"Phaaji, it's getting bright, but the sun isn't showing up on the horizon," Sid wondered as the clock struck 6 a.m., with no signs of the sun breaking over the horizon.

"Why isn't the sun coming out? The sky is clear," Sameer wondered as well.

After thinking for a moment, it finally clicked for them that Goa is a westward beach town, so one can only witness the sunset on the west side.

"Damn, the sun doesn't rise from the horizon in west coast towns," Sid exclaimed as they both burst out laughing at their ignorance.

They woke Harsha and hesitantly broke the news to her that the sunrise wouldn't be visible there.

True to her name, Harsha, an always happy soul, responded, "It's okay. I just enjoyed this night so much. Being happy with you is all that matters to me. Let's go back to the hotel."

"This has been one of the best times of my life," Sameer expressed.

"Mine too," replied Harsha, looking into his eyes.

"How lovely would it be to spend our special days together in Goa like this, in a beach shack by the seaside?" Sameer wished, unknowingly that the Almighty was listening to his wish at that very moment.

In the years to follow, the Almighty would mysteriously create opportunities for them to be in Goa during their wedding anniversaries.

21
Placements, Convocation & The Last Kiss!

In the last few months at the institution, the energy gradually shifted from pure academic rigor to preparations for placement interviews. Countless companies began visiting the campus, and every student was rushing from one company presentation to another. Anxious butterflies flitted in everyone's stomachs as they wondered which company would offer them a job in the coming weeks.

Students busily attended presentations and submitted their resumes. They experienced a rollercoaster of emotions: from being shortlisted at times to frequently not making the cut. They navigated the interview stage only to feel disappointed when they didn't progress to a good company's final round.

Deep down, everyone believed they would eventually secure a good start with some company.

Sameer had already accepted a job offer from the company where he completed his internship, so he was not part of the placement process. Although he had a desire to explore the various job opportunities available on campus, accepting the first offer he received kept him from doing so.

Sid dreamed of working at the Birla Group, even though the odds were stacked against him, given that around a hundred companies were visiting the campus.

"Phaaji, I just want to work with the Birla Group. That is my dream," Sid repeatedly told Sameer.

"Of all the companies visiting the campus, why only Birla? There are many other companies to compete for, and even more lucrative brands. Why get fixated on Birla?" Sameer tried to reason with him.

"I don't know, but I feel an unexplainable pull towards the Birla Group. It's my dream to work with them," Sid always reiterated.

As luck would have it, the divine forces aligned to make Sid's wish come true. Out of all the companies where he applied, he was selected by the Birla Group, and his joy knew no bounds. He rushed out of the interview room, where Sameer, Harsha, and others waited eagerly outside the hall.

"I received the offer from Birlas!" an ecstatic Sid exclaimed in disbelief.

At the same time, many prestigious multinational companies were also on campus that week. Harsha's remarkable academic record allowed her to be shortlisted by several of them. With Sameer exempt from the placement process, he focused entirely on helping her prepare for her interviews.

He conducted countless mock interview sessions, covering a plethora of common questions typically asked in such interviews.

After narrowly missing out on offers from the first few companies on campus, Harsha went for IBM, a prestigious company to aspire to. After a few rounds of interviews, she rushed out with the offer letter in hand. It was one of the happiest days of their lives. Tears of joy streamed down their faces as they instantly called their families to share the good news.

"I have one more important thing to share with you," Harsha said to Sameer.

"What? Now I'm curious," Sameer replied, eager to hear.

"They've offered me a role in the Training department," she exclaimed excitedly.

The two celebrated their joy, both having received offers in the same department at their respective companies.

"This is so uncanny; this definitely feels like divine intervention. We are meant to be together and share more of our lives with each other," Sameer said joyfully.

Very few offers were extended to students in the Training department, and Harsha and Sameer happened to be among that rare group.

The next few weeks flew by, and it was finally the day of convocation. Dressed in their best formal attire, complete with graduation gowns and caps, everyone's families gathered to witness this important milestone. It was a moment to cherish for the rest of their lives. Amidst the crowd of parents, Harsha and Sameer took a moment for themselves and asked Sid to quickly snap a picture of them in their graduation attire.

Just as many parents met each other on this momentous day, so too did the parents of Harsha and Sameer.

After receiving their postgraduate degrees, they realized that their time together in this haven of education had finally come to an end. On one hand, they were excited for a new beginning as their careers were about to take off; on the other hand, there was sadness at the thought of this chapter closing.

It was the last evening on campus before they would pack up and leave the next day.

"One last evening stroll on campus?" the boy texted.

"Yes, yes Bobo," the girl replied instantly.

Hand in hand, they walked around the campus for hours, not wanting the night to end. They fell into a comfortable silence, lost in reflection as mixed emotions swirled around them.

"Oh, I'm going to miss us on this campus so much," the girl said.

"I'm still processing that this is all ending tonight," the boy replied.

"How will we go about things from tomorrow?" the girl asked.

The two discussed how they would meet once a week until they started their jobs in different cities in a month.

"It's going to be hard not seeing you every day from tomorrow," the girl said, tears in her eyes.

"We'll find our way, Bebo. Remember, meeting is joy, parting is sorrow; this too shall pass, and we shall be together tomorrow," the boy reassured her with his favorite line as they shared one last kiss on campus, sitting on their favorite bench at the end of the street.

22

The Big Day of Our Fate

"Hey, my joining letter just came in," the girl texted.

Not wasting any time in suspense, the boy called immediately to hear her out.

"Which city?" asked the boy directly.

"Gurgaon," responded the girl.

Sameer had already received his appointment letter and joining dates. He was set to go to Bangalore to join the organization in a month. Now, Harsha had received her appointment for Gurgaon.

"There is one more update," the girl said.

"What is that now?" the boy asked, curious and hoping for a happy surprise in her voice.

"For the first month, I will be in Bangalore for my initial training, and then I will join the Gurgaon office," the girl disclosed.

"Yay!" the boy screamed in excitement, mirroring the girl's enthusiasm.

"A boy and a girl, both independent and adults, alone in a new city. Doesn't it sound like a risky proposition?" the boy joked.

"I think we should inform our parents. The time has come," responded the girl.

"I agree! Finally, we have arrived at that bridge we said we would cross when we reached it," the boy said.

"But I am scared," the girl admitted.

"Scared of what, Bebo?" the boy inquired.

"What if the outcome doesn't turn in our favor? What if there is resistance from our families? What if I am held back from meeting you in Bangalore, or worse, not even allowed to go there?" the girl poured out her concerns.

"Well, we are in this together. Even if there is resistance, we shall hold our ground. Remember, I am the long-haul guy! I will be with you for as long as it takes for things to turn in our favor, and they will," assured the boy.

"So, how do we go about it?" the girl asked.

"I will discuss it openly with my parents today and seek their guidance. The boy suggested.

His parents had met Harsha a couple of times in college and over dinner at their place which they had hosted for his friends. They had heard a lot about Harsha from him.

"I know they are very supportive; I will hear them out and update you," the boy shared his action plan.

As Sameer spoke with his parents, his father offered to take the lead.

"There is nothing to hide, nothing to fear. I will invite her dad over for coffee tomorrow and talk to him transparently. I am hopeful that he will understand and show support. After all, parents want their children to be happy, and you both are at your happiest when together. What more can we ask for?" his dad said confidently with a smile.

"Hey, what did you say to your dad?" Harsha called up, curious.

"Nothing much; I just poured my heart out to my parents. They expressed their support and happiness for us. My dad said he would call your dad for coffee one of these days to discuss it," Sameer explained.

"Well, he has already called him and invited him for tomorrow," she updated.

"What? Really that fast?" Sameer was surprised.

"Yes, my dad asked me about my feelings for you," Harsha added.

"Whoa, what did you say?" Sameer asked.

"I was a bit scared, but I held my nerves and confirmed my choice for us," Harsha replied.

"But my parents are feeling pressure about what to do and say in tomorrow's meeting. They're surprised that we didn't disclose our feelings for each other until now. My mom, in particular, is struggling to process this big news and sudden invitation. She thinks it's all happening too quickly and feels unprepared," Harsha explained.

The two secretly shared updates about their respective parents with each other.

"They're having a long conversation, planning what to do and say tomorrow. My mom wants my dad to hear your father out and take time to respond, rather than committing to anything on the spot. I'm worried," Harsha shared.

"Okay, we've done everything we could at this moment. Let's hope for the best tomorrow. It's in their hands now. Good night, and sleep well, dear," Sameer comforted his beloved.

"Sam, congratulations! We're all set. I just met your future father-in-law, and he also supported yours and Harsha's alliance. He will discuss it with his family, and we'll soon set a date for your Roka (a pre-engagement ceremony). Love you, beta. I'm leaving the place now, but I wanted to share this update with you first," Sameer's father said, delivering the happiest news over the phone.

Sameer hugged his mom and broke into tears upon hearing this news. "Is it really happening this quickly and easily? I'm still in disbelief. You parents are the best," he said.

While he wanted to share the news with Harsha immediately, he restrained himself, waiting for her to hear the update from her father directly.

A few hours later, the phone rang. Sameer eagerly picked up the call he had been waiting for. "We've crossed the bridge, Bobo," his beloved shared, her voice filled with happy tears.

She explained that everyone at her home was still in shock about how quickly their alliance was blessed. While her dad was convinced, happy, and satisfied, her mom was still struggling to digest the news.

"Is she not supportive of our alliance?" Sameer asked.

"She is, and she will eventually come to terms with today's big update. But she's upset with my dad for agreeing so quickly. She didn't anticipate that he would come back from one meeting with a lifelong commitment. She's still discussing it with him," Harsha narrated.

"That's understandable; it's such big news, and everything has unraveled for them in the last 24 hours. We should have kept them informed about our feelings for each other or at least given them some hints along the way," Sameer reflected.

"Anyhow, let's give them some time to absorb this news. But how do you feel, Mr. Nagi? Will you be my lawfully wedded husband?" Harsha asked, filled with love and excitement.

"I was your knight in shining armor, and now I am excited to be the king of your heart forever. I love you so much, Harsha... Will you be the queen of my heart?" the boy asked.

"Yes, yes, and yes—forever yours. I love you too, darling," the girl replied lovingly.

23

To a New Beginning!

The next year was fast, action-packed, adventurous, and marked the beginning of a new phase of life. Before the boy moved to Bangalore, the parents lovingly conducted a function named Roka, a pre-engagement ceremony. The joy of formally moving closer to each other forever was palpable.

The experience of moving to a new city, starting a new life in a new company, meeting new colleagues, and navigating unfamiliar surroundings was unsettling on one hand but also exciting on the other. There were new learnings, independent earnings, and the joy of seeing each other every other day during the first four weeks.

The two life companions worked diligently through the day and then met for dinner every evening in this new city. A few other friends from college would also join at times to reminisce about the golden times spent together in their institution.

Sharing an ice cream after every dinner became a daily ritual before the boy would drop her off at her guest house as he left for the company guest house provided for the first six weeks to him.

Once the girl returned to Gurgaon after her initial training period, the long distance between them put their relationship to the test. The missing touch of a hand, the lack of eye contact, and the absence of hugs were difficult to endure over voice calls. The two felt the void and incompleteness, and, unaware of the reason for their dissatisfaction, often incorrectly placed the blame on each other for the emptiness they were experiencing.

There were moments of extreme emotion, from the joy of receiving a love-filled, caring message to the pain and anguish of hanging up the phone after inconclusive, frustrated, mindless arguments.

The frustrations and anguish were severe, but they also felt temporary. When the dust settled overnight, the two would reconnect with a loving message the next morning as if nothing had happened.

Both were being trained to be trainers in their companies, and there was a lot they shared in common regarding their careers.

"I wish we could be in the same company, in the same department, doing the training that we both enjoy the most," the boy said.

"Yeah, maybe someday. I also feel excited about this field. The more programs I get certified to facilitate, the more fun it becomes," the girl replied.

"Okay, I can't live without you. I'm taking the flight tomorrow morning and will be in Delhi over the weekend. See you!" the boy declared, often throwing in surprises.

"Bobo, I have a surprise for you. I've been assigned to come to Bangalore for two days to train a group there," the girl would also frequently announce, as she actively sought training assignments in Bangalore every month.

"How do we get together in a city? It feels painful living through this long-distance relationship," Sameer asked.

"I am checking with my management about a transfer to Bangalore. They have a much larger base there, and it is likely possible in a few months," the girl shared with determination.

"I am also extensively looking for job opportunities at other companies in Gurgaon, but I have just started here, so it's too early for anything to materialize. My experience is insufficient for now," the boy sighed.

"Okay. Let's keep trying and see who gets lucky first," the girl said.

"And what if one of us moves to the other's city?" asked the boy.

"Then I will tell my parents that I want to marry this funny and caring fellow," she replied with a smile.

After a few months, the girl's request for a transfer to the Bangalore office was approved.

"Hey, guess what?" the girl asked over the call.

"What? Don't tell me your transfer to Bangalore has been approved!" the boy exclaimed as the girl confirmed.

It was a joyful evening for both as they shared the big news with their families.

"I think it's time to end this painful long-distance between us. Ms. Israni, what do you say? Are you ready, keen, and excited to marry this funny and caring fellow?" the boy proposed over the phone.

"Not just funny and caring, but also handsome and sometimes irritating too," the girl laughed.

"And yes, I want to be the queen of your heart and your partner for life, till death do us apart," the girl promised.

24
Wedding Bells!

After the Roka ceremony, the two got engaged in a beautiful event lovingly organized by their families. Their relationship began to grow beyond just the two of them as their bonds with each other's family members started to forge.

Both felt beautifully accepted, comfortable, and at home with each other's families. They bonded well with one another.

"So, April 7th it is!" Sameer's mom announced after a series of discussions among everyone to finalize the wedding date.

The next few months flew by quickly as they prepared for the big day.

"Good morning Bebo, your Bobo is ready to come and pick you up. And this time, it's going to be forever," read the boy's text on the morning of their wedding.

"Please delay a bit; my makeup artist is not done yet," smirked the girl.

The happiest days were also the busiest days. They passed by so quickly that they barely realized they were married.

"Wow! We are officially married now. Can you believe it?" exclaimed the boy.

"We've been waiting for this day for such a long time. We've been planning for it for months, and finally, it has happened," the girl shared in amazement.

The parents of the bride and groom worked joyfully and diligently to arrange the functions as envisioned by the couple. It was a happy union of two simple and loving families.

"They are all loving and caring, but I can't wait to have some time alone with you during our upcoming honeymoon," said the boy, struggling to find a private moment with his newlywed wife amid a house full of people.

"Just one more day of patience, my dear hubby. Starting tomorrow, it will just be the two of us. Not only in Nainital during our honeymoon, but also in Bangalore once we reach there," comforted the girl.

"Hope you won't get bored of me," she teased.

"You make me complete; how can complete be boring?" responded the boy, making a naïve attempt to impress his wife.

"Aww," the girl said, adoring his comment as they kissed and wrapped each other in their arms.

25

And they lived happily ever after! Or did they?

The dust from the functions in Delhi slowly settled as the couple embarked on their honeymoon—a beautiful trip to cherish for a lifetime.

Soon, they were off to Bangalore to begin their life together, finally.

Along with the euphoria of being together forever came the nagging behaviors and habits that surfaced. There was passionate love, but also some extreme disappointments arising from a few silly behaviors they discovered in each other.

However, the passion always outweighed the disappointments. The reasons to laugh and rejoice consistently surpassed the reasons to fight and argue. The phase of storming eventually gave way to a beautiful norming. They began to understand each other, made some changes for one another, and despite a few struggles, largely accepted each other.

Now, they would rekindle their shared love for looking at baby pictures.

"How's this one?" Sameer asked Harsha while showing her a picture of an adorable baby.

"Aww, she is so cute! I wish I had a larger image of this baby," replied Harsha. The very next day, Sameer brought home a large printout of that baby's image and pasted it on their wardrobe.

"They say that if you keep looking at a very cute baby's picture, you will be blessed with one," he informed her.

"Really? I hope it's true, as I want our baby to be just like her," Harsha replied.

During their first anniversary dinner, Sameer disclosed the big news to her.

"I finally got an offer from this major consulting company for a role in Gurgaon," he shared.

"Wow! Heartiest congratulations! I can't believe it's finally real—that we will shift to Delhi, close to both our parents," she replied.

"And the timing is perfect; I can now ask for a transfer to Delhi, having served the mandatory 12 months in my current role," she happily added.

"What better way to celebrate our first anniversary?" Sameer said.

The young couple moved to Delhi, and the day they landed in the capital, it felt like, "And they lived happily ever after."

Later that week, Harsha experienced excruciating pain in her abdomen. The painkillers were ineffective, so they consulted a doctor. It was diagnosed as appendicitis, and she needed to undergo surgery.

"Darling, good luck with your operation. I love you. While your surgery is underway, I'll go to the office for this unavoidable training program. By the time you wake up from the anaesthesia, I'll be right here next to you," Sameer told her, kissing her forehead as she was taken for the pre-surgery procedures.

Midway through the training, Sameer received a call from his father.

"Beta, the operation is going to take some more time. The doctors are doing their job, but I have some sad news to share."

His father delivered news that shattered Sameer's heart and left him numb. He wiped his tears and returned to the training to deliver the last section of the day. Afterward, he rushed to the hospital, struggling to hold back his tears...

And the story continues...